Why Me?
When Bad Things
Happen

Why Me?
When Bad Things Happen

Mike Aquilina

Our Sunday Visitor Publishing Division
Our Sunday Visitor, Inc.
Huntington, Indiana 46750

Nihil Obstat
Reverend Michael Heintz, Ph.D.
Censor Librorum

Imprimatur
✠ John M. D'Arcy
Bishop of Fort Wayne-South Bend
September 29, 2009

The *Nihil Obstat* and *Imprimatur* are official declarations that a book is free from doctrinal or moral error. It is not implied that those who have granted the *Nihil Obstat* and *Imprimatur* agree with the contents, opinions, or statements expressed.

The Scripture citations used in this work are taken from the *Second Catholic Edition of the Revised Standard Version of the Bible* (RSV), copyright © 1965, 1966, and 2006 by the Division of Christian Education of the National Council of the Churches of Christ in the United States of America. Used by permission. All rights reserved.

Every reasonable effort has been made to determine copyright holders of excerpted materials and to secure permissions as needed. If any copyrighted materials have been inadvertently used in this work without proper credit being given in one form or another, please notify Our Sunday Visitor in writing so that future printings of this work may be corrected accordingly.

ISBN: 978-1-59276-708-3 (Inventory No. T1029)
LCCN: 2009936902

Cover design by Rebecca J. Heaston
Cover art: Shutterstock
Interior design by Sherri L. Hoffman

PRINTED IN THE UNITED STATES OF AMERICA

Contents

"There's a woman who is embroidering. Her son, seated on a low stool, sees her work, but in reverse. He sees the knots of the embroidery, the tangled threads. He says, 'Mother, what are you doing? I can't make out what you are doing!' Then the mother lowers the embroidery hoop and shows the good part of the work. Each color is in place and the various threads form a harmonious design. So, we see the reverse side of the embroidery because we are seated on the low stool."

— St. Pio of Pietrelcina ("Padre Pio"),
ON FINDING MEANING IN SUFFERING

CHAPTER 1

Suffering Stinks

God sometimes allows us to be in such a profound darkness that not a single star shines in our skies.
— BLESSED CHARLES DE FOUCAULD

Somewhere a child died today. It was a long battle with cancer, or a terrible accident, or a battle between rival warlords — it doesn't matter. Somewhere today a mother is looking up to heaven with one question in her heart: *Why me?*

Why would God allow that kind of thing? Why would a mother have to lose her child? What kind of world is this, where everything that matters to you can be snatched away just like that?

Suffering is everywhere. Somewhere a man has just told his wife that he's leaving her. He's in love, he says, really in love for the first time in his life. He knows the woman is half his age, but she's his real soul mate.

And the wife who gave him fifteen years of her life can only look up to heaven and ask that same question: *Why me?*

Even in our ordinary daily lives, with nothing unusual going on, we suffer. We stub our toes, burn our fingers, get soaked by a car passing through a puddle. It's not big, spectacular suffering — we feel a bit silly even complaining about it.

But it's still suffering. And suffering stinks.

Why me?

We can think of plenty of people who deserve to suffer. How about bankers who give themselves millions in bonuses for running our banks into the ground? How about illegal arms dealers who profit off the misery of innocent victims of war? How about paramilitary bosses who press ten-year-old children into service in their never-ending wars for the sake of war?

Shouldn't they suffer instead of me?

We're always ready to find fault in other people, and we're always ready to excuse our own faults. But when we're honest with ourselves, we know that we aren't completely innocent either. We're all sinners.

Still, the punishments seem harsh.

Did I really do anything to deserve this?

Where It All Began

We know the story of Adam and Eve — how God told Adam and Eve not to eat the fruit of the Tree of the Knowledge of Good and Evil, and how Adam and Eve, persuaded by the wily serpent, went ahead and did it anyway. The Bible tells us that all the pain and suffering in the world came about as a result of that sin, as God explained to Adam and Eve when he found them hiding in the bushes like naughty schoolchildren:

> To the woman he said,
> "I will greatly multiply your pain in childbearing;

in pain you shall bring forth children,
yet your desire shall be for your husband,
 and he shall rule over you."
And to Adam he said,

"Because you have listened to the voice of your
 wife,
 and have eaten of the tree
of which I commanded you,
 'You shall not eat of it,'
cursed is the ground because of you;
 in toil you shall eat of it all the days of your
  life;
thorns and thistles it shall bring forth to you;
 and you shall eat the plants of the field.
In the sweat of your face
 you shall eat bread
till you return to the ground,
 for out of it you were taken;
you are dust,
 and to dust you shall return." (Gen 3:16–19)

Now, the Bible often uses "figurative language," meaning that some of the stories in it may be parables meant to teach us a moral truth rather than literal history. But the Church teaches that this story of Adam and Eve does literally refer to some kind of primordial event — a rejection of God that comes right at the beginning of human history.

We all have some reason to hide in the bushes from God.

So is that it, then? Is all the suffering in the world God's revenge for some disobedience our distant ancestors perpetrated — something we had nothing to do with?

That makes God sound kind of like a grouch.

Of course, anyone who's honest knows that sin didn't end with Adam and Eve. We can't say it often enough: we're all sinners. We all have some reason to hide in the bushes from God. We probably all deserve some kind of punishment.

Suffering as Punishment

Some people used to think — in fact, some people still think — that the world works on a simple system of rewards and punishments. Good people prosper, and any kind of suffering in this life is a punishment for sins. That was certainly a common view in Jesus' time. In fact, it was what Jesus' own disciples thought:

> As he passed by, he saw a man blind from his birth. And his disciples asked him, "Rabbi, who sinned, this man or his parents, that he was born blind?" Jesus answered, "It was not that this man sinned, or his parents, but that the works of God might be made manifest in him." (Jn 9:1–3)

The man was born blind — a misfortune, as the disciples thought, so it must be some form of punishment. But the world is a bit more complicated than that. Of course, Jesus gave the man his sight, and the story spread quickly: God, in Jesus, had made the imperfect perfect.

So here's a case where the suffering wasn't a punishment for sin at all. All our ordinary reasons don't work: there was no punishment involved. God had a different reason for allowing this man to be born blind. The healing showed the world, or at least anyone who was willing to pay attention, who this man Jesus really was.

Suffering is beginning to look like a very complicated subject.

Bad Things Happen to Good People

The book of Job is the greatest meditation on suffering in the Old Testament. Job is a blameless and upright man who always gives God his due. When he suffers, it's for what seems like no reason at all. In the story at the beginning, Satan makes a bet with God: Job praises God while he's prosperous, says Satan, but let him be miserable for a while and then he'll curse God, you just wait and see.

So Job's wealth, his family, and his health are all taken away from him, but he still doesn't curse God. That doesn't mean he doesn't complain.

Job's friends come by to tell him that he must have sinned somehow. Job answers them, knowing that he never did anything against God. But they persist: he must have sinned, because otherwise he wouldn't be suffering the way he is. He should repent, and God will remove the suffering.

Job's friends are allowed to make their very best arguments. They're not just straw men, set up to be knocked down by the mighty force of superior reason. Look at this one, for example:

"If you return to the Almighty and humble yourself,
    if you remove unrighteousness far from your
        tents,
if you lay gold in the dust,
    and gold of Ophir among the stones of the
        torrent bed,
and if the Almighty is your gold,
    and your precious silver;
then you will delight yourself in the Almighty,
    and lift up your face to God....
For God abases the proud,
    but he saves the lowly.
He delivers the innocent man;
    you will be delivered through the cleanness of
        your hands." (Job 22:23–26, 29–30)

Who could object to the advice that you should turn your back on gold and make God the object of your desire?

Yet Job's friend is wrong. Not because it isn't good to prize God above material things, not because it's wrong to repent, and not because God doesn't hear prayers. He's wrong because life just isn't so simple. You don't *know* that people are suffering because they sinned. Sometimes good people suffer. Sometimes bad people don't.

> *You don't know that people are suffering because they sinned.*

How can it be that way? Is God really so unfair? Or does it mean that

14

there is no God at all — that the universe is just random, and that nothing and nobody cares what happens to us?

These are the questions the book of Job asks — and they are the questions any thinking person has to ask about all the suffering in this world. Job is in a better position to ask them than most of us: he knows he's been a good man, whereas most of us know what awful sinners we are. But even a good man — or especially a good man — has to ask those questions.

Job never gets an answer to his questions, but he does get something most people who complain about their sufferings never do get: a visit from God himself. After Job is through arguing with his friends, God himself shows up to tell the friends they are wrong. But Job is wrong, too. He's wrong because he can't even *try* to understand the reasons for his own suffering. No one can understand the ways of God, as God himself tells Job from out of the whirlwind:

> "Where were you when I laid the foundation of
>   the earth?
>   Tell me, if you have understanding.
> Who determined its measurements — surely you
>   know!
>   Or who stretched the line upon it?
> On what were its bases sunk,
>   or who laid its cornerstone,
> when the morning stars sang together,
>   and all the sons of God shouted for joy?"

(Job 38:4–7)

Job simply has to admit that he doesn't understand and never can understand, because he doesn't have the key. But we do have the key. We do know somebody who was there at the moment of creation.

"In the beginning," John tells us, "was the Word."

Take Away

We don't understand why bad things happen to good people.

CHAPTER 2

The Paradox of Suffering

When it is all over, you will not regret having suffered; rather you will regret having suffered so little, and suffered that little so badly.

— BLESSED SEBASTIAN VALFRE

The People Who Suffer the Most

No one has to tell us that we hate suffering, and no one has to tell us that it's hard to understand. But we do sometimes notice something strange about suffering. Often the very best people we know — the kindest and happiest people — are the ones who've suffered the most.

The twentieth century was a century of epic villains and proportionally inspiring saints. Of all the villains, certainly the most reviled is Adolf Hitler, whose Nazi government turned Germany into a house of horrors. And of all the saints, few have inspired as many Christians as Maximilian Kolbe, one of the Nazis' millions of victims.

Father Maximilian Kolbe was a Polish priest who was caught in the horror of the Nazi occupation. As an amateur-radio broadcaster, he frequently denounced Nazi brutality. He published magazine articles condemning the occupation. It wasn't something you could easily do without getting arrested, and Father Kolbe was arrested in early 1941. He was sent to Auschwitz, the most notoriously horrible of the Nazi concentration camps.

The Nazis had a very effective system for discouraging escapes. If one person went missing, the guards would round up ten random prisoners from the same cell block and sentence them to die by starvation. If you tried to escape, you were condemning ten of your friends to death.

When one prisoner went missing from Father Kolbe's cell block, the guards did the usual roundup. They shut their ears to the expected pleas for mercy, but Father Kolbe heard one young man protesting that he had a wife and family.

Father Kolbe led the group in prayers and songs.

So Father Kolbe approached the guards and asked if they would take him instead. The guards were surprised, but they didn't object; they just needed ten bodies. The priest took the place of the condemned prisoner, and he went off with the rest to Block 13 to starve to death. There, according to prisoners who were assigned to sweep up the place, Father Kolbe led the group in prayers and songs. One by one the condemned men died, until Father Kolbe was the only one left. The guards finally lost patience and killed him by lethal injection.

What a horrible way to die! But here's the thing: all the accounts say that Father Kolbe was *happy*. Not that he leaped for joy, but he seemed perfectly confident and serene. He even died with an expression of deep peace on his face.

This doesn't even make any sense. Aren't you *supposed* to be miserable in a Nazi extermination cell?

Suffering and Happiness

But this is the paradox of suffering. Suffering — especially suffering with a purpose — doesn't necessarily make us unhappy.

In fact, the opposite sometimes seems to be true.

Think back on all the kindest, happiest, most serene people you've ever known. Chances are pretty good that they're also some of the people who've suffered the most.

Not many of them have spent time in a Nazi death camp. But they've had their trials. They're widows and widowers. They've lost children. They're cancer survivors, or people who aren't going to survive much longer.

Yet they seem to have a smile for us every time we see them. They're always thinking of ways to do little things for other people. Their faces light up with smiles at the least provocation. They love to play with the neighborhood children. We see joy in everything they do, as though somehow they know that all's right with the world.

How can they be happy? Is it possible that, in some way, the suffering helped them learn to be happy?

The Purpose of Pain

We do have to be careful here. On the one hand, it's beginning to look as though suffering can be a good thing. On the other hand, God gave us the instinct to avoid pain for a reason. Self-preservation is a good thing.

That's what pain is for. It's a marvelous gift, when you think about it. We're lazy — there's no use denying it. Even when we know something is good for us, we won't necessarily get out of our chairs and do it. Why do we see so many stories about how we all need more exercise? It's because it's just easier to sit in our chairs and do nothing, even when we know it would be better for us to get up and go.

Pain makes us do what we have to do to survive.

But when it's a matter of life and death — when we need immediate action to save ourselves — then we do it. Why? Because it *hurts* if we don't.

That's why pain is really a gift from God. If we didn't have it, the human race would just die out. Pain makes us do what we have to do to survive.

Even our mental anguish has a purpose. It hurts to lose someone we love — so we protect the ones we love. We raise our children to adulthood through twenty long years or so, precisely because we love them so much and can't bear to see anything bad happen to them.

Well, we might think, *that's all very well to say. But what does God really know about this so-called gift he's given us? Does he know how much pain hurts?*

The answer is that he knows better than anybody.

Take Away

Suffering can help us learn to be happy.

CHAPTER 3

Jesus, Our Companion in Suffering

Life himself came down to be slain; Bread came down to suffer hunger; the Way came down to endure weariness on his journey; the Fountain came down to experience thirst. Do you, then, refuse to work and to suffer?
— ST. AUGUSTINE OF HIPPO

In human history, no one has suffered more than Jesus Christ. But there's good news for us in the bad things that Jesus suffered: "For because he himself has suffered and been tempted, he is able to help those who are tempted" (Heb 2:18). That's the message of the cross: our suffering isn't hopeless, and our temptation isn't unmanageable, because Jesus is going through all of this with us.

Jesus' Mental Anguish

But how did Jesus suffer? When we think of the suffering of Christ, we think of the Passion — the events leading up to the Crucifixion and the Crucifixion itself. But the Gospels tell us a lot more about Jesus' suffering that we don't usually think about. Jesus didn't just suffer physical pain at the end of his life. Throughout his earthly career, he had to deal with the kind of mental pain we all suffer: the pain of loss, or of rejection, or — above all — of seeing the people we love suffer.

Jesus had to deal with the kind of mental pain we all suffer.

Look closely at the story of Lazarus, the brother of Mary and Martha. These three were some of Jesus' best friends. Remember that Jesus had been some distance away when he heard that Lazarus had died, but he went back to Judea even though he knew the authorities were after him:

> Now Jesus had not yet come to the village, but was still in the place where Martha had met him. When the Jews who were with her in the house, consoling her, saw Mary rise quickly and go out, they followed her, supposing that she was going to the tomb to weep there. Then Mary, when she came where Jesus was and saw him, fell at his feet, saying to him, "Lord, if you had been here, my brother would not have died." When Jesus saw her weeping, and the Jews who came with her also weeping, he was deeply moved in spirit and troubled; and he said, "Where have you laid him?" They said to him, "Lord, come and see." Jesus wept. (Jn 11:30–35)

Stop and meditate on what must be the most profound single verse in the whole Bible. It's the shortest verse, too — just two words in English: "Jesus wept."

Jesus Suffers With Us

We know that the most unbearable sufferings are mental rather than physical. The pain of losing an arm is not to be compared with the pain of losing a child.

And far worse than our own suffering is the suffering of someone we love. What father wouldn't wish to take all the pain on himself if only he could take it away from his child? What daughter wouldn't do the same for her mother?

So if we look closer, we see that Jesus didn't weep when he heard Lazarus had died. No, it wasn't the death that affected Jesus. It was the unbearable sadness of his friends, the people he loved.

Jesus wasn't pretending to cry to make a point. He was suffering the same grief, the same anguish that we feel when someone we love dearly is suffering. And it doesn't even matter if we know it's going to be all better soon: the more we love our friends and family, the more their sorrow makes us grieve, too.

Here's a mystery of mysteries, then, but also one of the most consoling things in the Bible. God himself took on human form and suffered everything we suffer. And it wasn't just the physical pain.

We can't complain that God doesn't understand, that he's too powerful to know what it feels like to be a simple grieving human. God understands our sorrow on the deepest and most personal level: so much so, that God himself wept for our grief. This is what the letter to the Hebrews was talking about: "Because he himself has suffered and been tempted, he is able to help those who are tempted."

We don't get out of grief and anguish. There is suffering in the world, and we will suffer with it.

But we won't do it alone — not if we remember that Jesus himself is right there beside us. Instead of despairing or grumbling, we can remember that Jesus is with us, sharing our suffering. In those two words, "Jesus wept," we have one of the greatest mysteries in the Bible, but also one of the greatest consolations. God *really does* understand what it's like. Jesus weeps with us.

Faith and Trust

We've spent a lot of time with the story of Lazarus precisely because it's *not* what we usually think about when we think about the suffering of Christ. But it's really one of the keys to understanding what Christ really suffered.

The physical pain of crucifixion is unimaginable, and that's certainly a big part of the suffering of Christ. But when Jesus saw our grief — our mental anguish — that was what made him break down in tears. That compassion, the grief he shared with us, was what made him go through with the Crucifixion itself. And because Jesus trusted his Father, incalculable good came from his suffering and death. He was showing us that good comes out of our suffering, if we're open to trusting God as he did. Consider with me Jesus' dying moments.

Just before he died, Jesus cried out, "My God, my God, why have you abandoned me?" (Mt 27:46 and Mk 15:34).

It sounds like a cry of despair. We read the Gospel story, and at this point we're frankly baffled. It sounds as though Jesus has given up hope. How is that possible?

The clouds start to clear when we realize that Jesus was quoting the first line of Psalm 22. Just the first line of a familiar song carries the whole meaning into our hearts, and the same thing was true back in Jesus' time. When the people Jesus knew heard the words of a favorite psalm, the whole meaning of it came rushing down on them.

They couldn't help understanding Psalm 22 as a prophecy of the Crucifixion. The details are a perfect match — right down to "they divide my garments among them, and for my clothing they cast lots" (Ps 22:18).

God turned our greatest evil into our greatest good.

All the pain, the suffering, the torture, and the humiliation of the Crucifixion are there in that psalm. But that's not the end of the story.

The psalm isn't about the pain and the torture. The psalm is about faith: faith that, although I'm suffering now, I'll be praising God for my deliverance in the future. The whole last third of that psalm is a song of praise, not a cry of despair. The psalmist confidently predicts, "Posterity shall serve him; men shall tell of the Lord to the coming generation, and proclaim his deliverance to a people yet unborn, that he has wrought it" (Ps 22:30–31).

This is the story of the cross. Jesus' death on the cross is a horror, a thing we still can't fit into our minds.

One perfect man came into the world and did nothing but good, and because of that we killed him.

But that isn't the end of the story. It's not even the middle. It's just the beginning.

God, who turns evil into good, turned our greatest evil into our greatest good. Not just in spite of Jesus' suffering, but *because of* Jesus' suffering, all of humanity has the chance to break that cycle of sin and death that trapped us into crucifying him in the first place. Jesus' death on the cross was not the tragic end of a wasted life, but the triumphant beginning of our own salvation.

We can become like Christ, rising triumphant from death, overcoming the sinful nature that ties us down to the world.

But to become like Christ, we have to suffer with Christ.

Take Away

Jesus supports us in our suffering and brings good from it.

CHAPTER 4

Suffering With Christ

Those who suffer for the love of God help Jesus carry his cross, and if they persevere, they will share his glory in heaven.

— St. Paul of the Cross

What It Means to "Take Up Your Cross"

If any man would come after me, let him deny himself and take up his cross and follow me" (Mt 16:24 and Mk 8:34).

That's what Jesus himself told us, and we repeat the phrase over and over without really stopping to think of what it means. Maybe we talk about something as "my cross to bear," like a grumpy coworker, when what we mean is "a thing that mildly annoys me."

What did Jesus really mean by "take up his cross"? We can understand this hard saying a bit better when we look at it in context:

From that time Jesus began to show his disciples that he must go to Jerusalem and suffer many things from the elders and chief priests and scribes, and be killed, and on the third day be raised. And Peter took him and began to rebuke him, saying, "God forbid, Lord! This shall never happen to you." But he turned and said to Peter, "Get behind me, Satan! You are a hindrance to me; for you are not on the side of God, but of men."

Then Jesus told his disciples, "If any man would come after me, let him deny himself and take up his cross and follow me." (Mt 16:21–24)

Now, Peter actually would end up being crucified. He literally did take up his cross many years later in Rome, when Nero was persecuting the Christians.

But it wasn't his unwillingness to die that earned Peter a rebuke from the Master. Peter probably was quite willing to fight and die to defend Jesus. Later on, he was the only one to draw a weapon when soldiers came to arrest Jesus in the Garden of Gethsemane.

No, the cross Peter wasn't willing to bear was losing his Master and friend without even putting up a fight. He loved his friend with all his heart, and he would rather die than lose him. Yet he would have to come to terms with losing Jesus; that was the plan, and Peter must not stand in the way of it.

Bearing All Losses

Now we have a good idea of what Jesus meant when he told us to take up our crosses. He wasn't just talking about physical pain or even death. He meant that we have to be prepared to lose everything we hold most dear — our mothers and fathers, our wives and husbands, or even our children, if it comes to that — and still trust that God's plan, no matter how incomprehensible it may seem to us, is working.

This trust is the hardest thing of all for us to learn. We think we know what makes us happy, and then suddenly God takes it away. How can we trust God after that?

How can I trust a God who takes away the job I counted on to feed my family? How can I trust a God who let my only child come down with a terrible disabling disease? How can I trust a God who would let my mother slowly lose her reason and her memory? How can I trust a God who would turn my life upside-down that way?

> *We have to be prepared to lose everything we hold most dear.*

How, Peter asks, could I trust a God who would take away the friend who finally made my life *mean* something?

Sharing in Christ's Suffering

Yet we need to learn to trust God. And the best way to grow in trust is to remember that when we suffer those pains of love, we're sharing the suffering of Christ.

> Blessed be the God and Father of our Lord Jesus Christ, the Father of mercies and God of all comfort, who comforts us in all our affliction, so that we may be able to comfort those who are in any affliction, with the comfort with which we ourselves are comforted by God. For as we share abundantly in Christ's sufferings, so through Christ we share abundantly in comfort too. (2 Cor 1:3–5)

Right here is one of the keys we need to open up the mystery of suffering. It's exactly the key that Job, who lived before Jesus Christ came into the world, didn't have and couldn't have: "As we share abundantly in Christ's sufferings, so through Christ we share abundantly in comfort too."

Christ didn't come to tell us that everything would be all right starting now. He actually told us that we were going to be suffering a lot more than we've already suffered. But we should rejoice in our suffering. Why? Because the suffering is leading us toward joy. It's teaching us how to be more like Christ.

This is why the suffering is worth it, no matter how hard it is at the moment. It really does help us become the kind of people God wants us to be — people who trust the Father the way Christ trusts the Father.

Learning Trust

God can't do anything for us if we don't trust him. And that trust isn't easy to learn.

Christ was literally perfection in human form: God incarnate as a human being.

Yet even Jesus the man had to learn. The Son of God had accepted our human limitations; as Jesus of Nazareth, he would live a human life, with human growth in body and mind: "And Jesus increased in wisdom and in stature, and in favor with God and man" (Lk 2:52).

That's one of the great mysteries of the Incarnation: that Jesus Christ, the omniscient God, as a human had to "increase in wisdom."

But how did he learn? Certainly he was taught the Scriptures, so well that by the age of twelve he was astounding the greatest teachers in Jerusalem (see Lk 2:46–47). But more than just book learning was necessary. The letter to the Hebrews puts it strikingly, and warns us that it's a deep mystery:

> Although he was a Son, he learned obedience through what he suffered; and being made perfect he became the source of eternal salvation to all who obey him.... (Heb 5:8–9)

Jesus "learned obedience through what he suffered." That's really an astonishing thing to say. Although he was truly God, he was also truly a man. Jesus the man had to learn to trust God, and he learned it by suffering.

Jesus the man had to learn to trust God.

God *does* bring good out of our suffering — even if it seems impossible to believe now. What good, Peter demanded, could possibly come out of the authorities killing his friend and Master? What good could possibly come out of Nazis torturing a poor Polish priest to death?

Good News About Suffering

Yet we know that good *did* come. We know that because we have hindsight — we can look back at the past. We know that the way to salvation led through the cross. We know that a Polish family was reunited, and that generations of Christians have been inspired to joyful self-denial, because of one priest's sacrifice.

31

Our experiences now are teaching us to have trust in the future as well as confidence in the past.

Jesus knows how hard it is to learn that trust. Sharing our human nature, he had to learn it for himself. And because Jesus came to share our nature, now we share God's nature. We're God's own people, and we become like Christ.

This is the great news about suffering. By *suffering* like Christ, we can *become* like him — if we learn the lessons our suffering can teach us.

To live a truly divine life, we must follow the way that Jesus marked out for us. His way was a way of suffering. But it was not a way of despair and misery, and ours doesn't have to be either. Once we know that there's a *purpose* to our suffering — that it's leading us somewhere — then no suffering can really conquer us. If we follow Jesus, we are not losing our lives, but laying them down. Like Jesus, we're giving consent to God's will. Remember what Jesus told his disciples about losing his life:

> "No one takes it from me, but I lay it down of my own accord. I have power to lay it down, and I have power to take it again; this charge I have received from my Father." (Jn 10:18)

We lay down our lives with Jesus, and with Jesus we'll take them up again.

That's what it means to take up our crosses. We lay down our lives — everything we've planned for and everything we've hoped for — and accept the suffering that comes to us. We endure our trials patiently, even joyfully, because we know that they're only the route to something unimaginably glorious. Suffering is the way to our final destiny.

And what is that final destiny? Nothing less than to be, in Jesus Christ, daughters and sons of God ourselves.

Take Away

Enduring suffering trains us to trust God and makes us like Christ.

CHAPTER 5

Children of God

As iron is fashioned by the fire and on an anvil, so in the fire of suffering and under the weight of trials, our souls receive the form that our Lord desires for them to have.

— ST. MADELEINE SOPHIE BARAT

Becoming Children of God

When we say "Son of God," we know we're talking about Jesus Christ.

We're also used to talking about ourselves, and about everyone else in the world, as "God's children." But we tend to think of it as a metaphor when we apply the phrase to ourselves.

Yet it's so much more than that. When we say we are children of God, we can mean it in the most literal, metaphysical, and genealogical way.

How can that be?

It happens because we're united to Christ. He is the only begotten Son of God. His sonship is eternal. But the Son of God became the Son of Man so that the children of men might become children of God. By taking up our human life, he came to share his own divine life with us. St. Peter says that he made us "partakers of the divine nature" (2 Pet 1:4). And as St. Paul explains, he gave us the Holy Spirit, who makes us truly the children of God:

> For you did not receive the spirit of slavery to fall back into fear, but you have received the spirit of sonship. When we cry, "Abba! Father!" it is the Spirit himself bearing witness with our spirit that we are children of God, and if children, then heirs, heirs of God and fellow heirs with Christ, provided we suffer with him in order that we may also be glorified with him. (Rom 8:15–17)

We are heirs of God. Everything that belongs to God belongs to us, just as it belongs to God's own Son.

Our Inheritance in Christ

Think about that for a moment. What belongs to God? Well, everything. All goodness, all joy, all love — it all belongs to God. That's what we stand to inherit.

But there's a condition: Paul says that we're fellow heirs with Christ "provided we suffer with him in order that we may also be glorified with him."

Our suffering is part of God's plan.

Christ's route to glory led through suffering. Even though he prayed, "Father, if you are willing, remove this cup from me," he immediately added, "nevertheless not my will, but yours, be done" (Lk 22:42). We need to be ready with the same prayer. Sometimes our suffering is part of God's plan in a way we can't understand at the moment. It may be that we need to suffer in order to "put to death the deeds of the body" (Rom 8:13) — to detach ourselves from the things of this world where we've mistakenly put all our hope.

But the rewards are worth it. As St. Paul says:

> I consider that the sufferings of this present time are not worth comparing with the glory that is to be revealed to us. For the creation waits with eager longing for the revealing of the sons of God.... We know that the whole creation has been groaning with labor pains together until now; and not only the creation, but we ourselves, who have the first fruits of the Spirit, groan inwardly as we wait for adoption as sons, the redemption of our bodies. (Rom 8:18–19, 22–23)

Here Paul uses a striking metaphor that makes us sit up and take notice. All of creation suffers — we can see that. But the sufferings are like labor pains.

The Labor Pains of New Birth

Now, any mother will tell you that labor pains can be some of the most excruciating pains any human has ever felt. Giving birth hurts, as God had warned Adam and Eve that it would.

But we greet labor with joy, because a new life is coming into the world. No one pities or mourns for a mother who has just given birth. Everyone congratulates her, and the mother herself radiates joy.

Maybe this whole question of suffering is beginning to make a bit of sense. If we can only see that our suffering has a purpose, then we can approach it with the same joy we see in a mother who's about to give birth. That doesn't mean we won't cry out in pain, but they'll be labor pains, and we can endure them and even celebrate them because they lead to life.

Keeping our minds focused on that new life is what the Christian virtue of hope is for. We can't see the new life ahead of us, just as a laboring mother can't see the baby until the birth. But hope can keep us going. As St. Paul says, "We know that in everything God works for good with those who love him, who are called according to his purpose" (Rom 8:28).

We always say that the Lord works in mysterious ways, but when we suffer we have a hard time believing it. But actually, that's when we can be most sure that God is working for our good.

The Ground of Our Hope

Paul teaches us that God destined us for glory — and part of that glorification is being "conformed to the image of his Son" (Rom 8:29). We should look at a cruci-fix when we read those words. That's the image of God's Son, showing the infinite love that God wants to share with all of us.

> *God is working for our good.*

So if God is always working for our good, then even the bad things that happen to us are part of his plan for good. This is where we need to work on our faith, but we can see now that it must be true. If

God is really on our side, then there can't be anything strong enough to take away our ultimate happiness:

> What then shall we say to this? If God is for us, who is against us? He who did not spare his own Son but gave him up for us all, will he not also give us all things with him? Who shall bring any charge against God's elect? It is God who justifies; who is to condemn? Is it Christ Jesus, who died, yes, who was raised from the dead, who is at the right hand of God, who indeed intercedes for us? Who shall separate us from the love of Christ? Shall tribulation, or distress, or persecution, or famine, or nakedness, or peril, or sword? As it is written,
>
>> "For your sake we are being killed all the day long;
>
>> we are regarded as sheep to be slaughtered."
>
> No, in all these things we are more than conquerors through him who loved us. For I am sure that neither death, nor life, nor angels, nor principalities, nor things present, nor things to come, nor powers, nor height, nor depth, nor anything else in all creation, will be able to separate us from the love of God in Christ Jesus our Lord. (Rom 8:31–39)

This is the ground of our hope. God's love transcends every other power. Nothing that has happened, nothing that is happening now, and nothing that will ever happen can separate us from that love. Even the things we fear the most — wars, plagues, cancer, murder — can't come between us and the love of God.

In baptism we entered Christ's life, death, and resurrection. He has shared it with us, with the pledge of his glory.

We are children of God. We live in Christ. We live with Christ's life. We live out the life of Christ. Our heavenly Father wills us to be ever more like his only-begotten — ever more to be Christ.

God's revelation is more than a disclosure of information. It's a sharing of life — the Word was made flesh for this purpose. Once we see that, we know that our suffering is making us more like Christ. It's another Christian paradox: our mourning is the reason for our rejoicing.

Take Away

Suffering with the purpose of becoming like Christ leads to joy.

CHAPTER 6

Rejoicing in Suffering

Suffering borne in the will quietly and patiently is a continual, very powerful prayer before God.
— ST. JANE FRANCES DE CHANTAL

We're all going to die. This should arrive as news to nobody.

But if we must die, and suffer in dying, we should wish to die as St. Maximilian Kolbe did. Not that we have to undergo the horrors of starvation and thirst, but we should know how to die at peace, to die happy. To do this we must learn to *live* at peace and be happy, even though we must suffer.

How can we do that? How can we learn not just to endure our suffering, but to accept it with joy?

First, we can learn to be thankful. Cultivate the habit of gratitude. Set aside a time every day — maybe just before dinner, maybe just before you go to bed — to be thankful for what you have. Not just in general terms: *list* the things you're thankful for. For example, you could thank the Lord for your birth, for creating you in his image, for making you his daughter or son at your baptism, for your parents, your brothers and sisters, your spouse, your children, your grandchildren, your friends, your vocation, your job or school, your gifts (both natural and spiritual), for his provision for your well-being, for his forgiveness of your sins, and much more.

It will be easy to do when things are going right. But if you develop the habit, you'll be surprised how many things you can think of even when things are going wrong.

Psychological research has demonstrated that this simple exercise is very effective in reducing stress levels, adjusting attitude, and even achieving positive life goals. Gratitude shifts our focus from what we lack to what we have. It also draws our attention to the times we are on the receiving end of simple kindnesses, from friends and neighbors and family members. Over time, we realize how much we receive in life. And thus, we grow in humility as well, recognizing our dependence on others, but especially on God.

All of these are benefits in the natural order, but they provide a solid foundation for spiritual growth. We know this from one of the very basic tenets of Catholic theology: grace does not destroy nature, but builds on it and perfects it. Gratitude is a good, natural, and psychological habit that can be raised up into a virtue with real spiritual and supernatural power.

We feel much better when we help others.

Second, we can practice *giving*. We don't have to die for anybody — not just yet. But little kindnesses go a long way. It's surprising how much better we *feel* when we're helping others, not just thinking of ourselves.

Some people experience healing through volunteering. For example, serving the homeless, the abused, or the hungry can wrench us out of our self-pity and confront us with the sufferings of others. We "suffer with" them — that's the root meaning of the word *compassion*. When we relieve their pain, even just a little, we sometimes gain a sense of satisfaction and fulfillment.

If we are so incapacitated that we cannot donate time to charitable causes, we can still compose a program of giving. We can write letters or e-mails of encouragement to people who are lonely or struggling. We can call family members, planning in advance a few positive things to say (including our promise of prayers).

No matter how little we have, we can always find something to give.

Third, we can "offer up" our sufferings for the sake of others. Pope Benedict XVI urged everyone to take up this practice in his encyclical letter *Spe Salvi*.

Since we truly share in the life of Christ, our suffering is like his own: It has true redemptive value. It can save others — if we make the offering, as he did — if we give ourselves, with all our pain, as he did.

St. Paul put it well: "In my flesh I complete what is lacking in Christ's afflictions for the sake of his body, that is, the church" (Col 1:24). Now, what could be lacking in Christ's sufferings? Only what he willed to be lacking, so that we could take it on as our own.

It's a basic Christian principle that has been proven repeatedly. We all marvel at the accomplishments of Blessed Mother Teresa of Calcutta and the active works of the religious order she founded, the Missionaries of Charity. But Mother Teresa herself often gave credit to Jacqueline de Decker, even going so far as to call her the real foundress of the order.

Who was Jacqueline de Decker? She was a severely disabled Belgian woman, confined to bed much of the time, suffering in a body cast and enduring countless surgeries and bone grafts. But she didn't let her suffering go to waste. She offered it up, as Christ did on the cross, and she lived to see the fruit of her suffering. De Decker founded an organization called the Sick and Suffering Co-Workers of the Missionaries of Charity, men and women who see their pains and trials as a real *labor*, a true cooperation in the life of the missionaries. She outlived Mother Teresa by almost twelve years.

Another great spiritual writer, Elisabeth Leseur, suffered from cancer, but even more from the atheism and anti-Catholicism of her husband. But she offered the pain and humiliations of her disease for the sake of her husband's conversion. In time, her husband not only returned to the faith, but even became a Dominican priest.

I can add my own testimony to the effectiveness of such prayer. When we married, my wife, Terri, was not Catholic and she made it clear that she never would be. It was not in the realm of possibility. Then, one summer day in 1990, my parish priest suffered a severe injury and had to undergo emergency surgery. I called him in the hospital, and he told me that he was offering all the pain for Terri's conversion. I didn't mention any of this to Terri. But the next day we were out for a walk when she suddenly announced that she had decided to become Catholic.

Our suffering is indeed a powerful form of prayer, when we want it to be, and when we *will* it to be, when we unite it with the suffering of Christ.

Jesus' Instructions for a Happy Life

Meanwhile, we can keep praying. Jesus himself never hesitated to call on his Father for help, and we shouldn't hesitate either. Though we can't understand God's plan sometimes, the closer we are to God, the easier it is to trust in his wisdom.

Fortunately, we're not left without guidance here. Jesus himself gave us some very specific instructions for living a happy life.

> "Blessed are the poor in spirit, for theirs is the kingdom of heaven....
>
> "Blessed are those who are persecuted for righteousness' sake, for theirs is the kingdom of heaven.
>
> "Blessed are you when men revile you and persecute you and utter all kinds of evil against you falsely on my account. Rejoice and be glad, for your reward is great in heaven, for so men persecuted the prophets who were before you." (Mt 5:3, 10–12)

So you should be happy when everyone makes fun of you, or when people are saying nasty things about you, or when they're throwing you in prison because of what you believe.

It sounds like a rotten sort of happiness. But it isn't.

If we've learned anything at all from our suffering — and we've all suffered, and we'll all suffer more — it ought to be that *circumstances* don't make us happy. That's the lesson suffering has to teach us. And it's the hardest lesson we'll ever learn.

From the beginning, we've always thought *things* would make us happy. Adam and Eve had everything anyone could possibly want, but they were convinced by the world's first professional marketer that, if only they had that one fruit, their lives would be just perfect.

But the first thing Jesus tells us is "Blessed are the poor in spirit." People who don't put their trust in things or circumstances to make them happy are the ones who really know how to be happy — "for theirs is the kingdom of heaven."

The Path to Glory

The kingdom of heaven is the source of all true happiness. Love, the self-giving love that Jesus followed straight to the cross, is the only thing that really makes us happy. But in order to have that happiness, we need to learn how to let go of *things* — the circumstances of our earthly life that we count on to make us happy.

No matter how careful we are, eventually we're going to have to let go of them, every one of them. House, car, family, friends — we have to say good-bye to them all sometime, because we're all going to die.

That's why we should rejoice to share Christ's sufferings: not because we're part of some strange masochistic sect whose members like to beat themselves up, but because those sufferings are leading us to glory, just as Jesus' sufferings were his path to glory.

> Beloved, do not be surprised at the fiery ordeal which comes upon you to prove you, as though something strange were happening to you. But rejoice in so far as you share Christ's sufferings, that you may also rejoice and be glad when his glory is revealed. (1 Pet 4:12–13)

Is Peter actually telling us we should be *happy* to be suffering? Yes, he is, and that's what we have to learn. If we endure it with a good heart, remembering that suffering is for a *purpose*, then suffering is *teaching us to be happy*.

Happiness Takes Work

That's because happiness is a skill. It's not something that's either given to you or taken away from you by the world, or even by God. God wants you to be happy — in fact, it's the reason he made you. But he has to teach you how to do it. Sometimes the exercises are painful — learning anything takes work. But they're necessary, because the alternative is misery forever.

A while ago, when markets were crashing and the wealth of the world was evaporating before our eyes, there was a story in the papers about a billionaire who had killed himself. He had lost everything in the crash.

Well, not quite everything. It turned out that what he had left would have been more money than just about anybody we know will ever see in a lifetime. The man had killed himself because otherwise he would be reduced to living as a mere millionaire, and that was an unimaginable hardship to him.

We shake our heads at that poor man, wondering how anyone could possibly be so greedy that he'd rather die than be reduced to a mere millionaire. But most of us are just as greedy. We don't have as much to be greedy about, but we're just as despondent if what we have is taken away.

The Power of Thankfulness

"For whoever would save his life will lose it; and whoever loses his life for my sake and the gospel's will save it" (Mk 8:35).

That idea is so important that it appears six times in all of the Gospels: once each in Mark and John, and twice each in Matthew and Luke. The people who knew Jesus must have remembered it as something he was always saying.

We have to lose everything to gain even more.

We have to give ourselves away to find ourselves. We have to lose everything to gain even more. We're destined for heaven, but if we cling to earthly things — even the best earthly things — we'll never get there.

We're thinking about things the wrong way. When we go down our checklist of things to be thankful for, we should remember to be *thankful* for our hardships.

At first, it will be hard to do without a grimace or a sneer. The sarcasm in our heads will be practically deafening. "Oh, yes, thank you *so much* for taking away my job. I *really* appreciate that."

But remember that Jesus himself learned obedience through what he suffered. The things we suffer are hard to deal with, but they're our lessons in taking up our cross. They're teaching us how to be *really* happy, not just superficially or temporarily happy.

Instead of *getting*, we need to focus our attention on *giving*. That's what really leads to happiness. It's what heaven is like: complete, joyous self-giving, always and forever. We can practice that way of life now — and then, in spite of all our suffering, and maybe even because of it, we can taste a little bit of heaven right here on earth.

So have we answered the question "Why me?"?

In some ways we'll never have a complete answer, because we'll never know God's whole plan until we're with God. But we have a pretty good general answer now. God wants to make us more like Jesus, so we can be ready for a life of eternal joy and love.

God designed us and destined us for happiness. But because we have free will, without which there can be no love, we have the power to choose the wrong over the right, to abandon God and chase the things that can never really make us happy.

Ultimately, if we choose God, our destiny is to be his sons and daughters, sisters and brothers of Jesus Christ, inheriting the kingdom of heaven itself, knowing the unspeakable joy of unlimited love.

God wants us all to know that joy — the same joy the Trinity, eternally loving and eternally giving, has always known. It won't be easy getting there. Sometimes we'll sweat drops like blood. Sometimes we'll weep and mourn. But the joy is there, waiting for us, and — if we have faith — our suffering is leading us to it.

Take Away

When bad things happen, don't ask "Why me?" but look for the good that the Lord will bring from your suffering.

Readings and Prayers
in Times of Trial

Hope in God's Love

Therefore, since we are justified by faith, we have peace with God through our Lord Jesus Christ. Through him we have obtained access to this grace in which we stand, and we rejoice in our hope of sharing the glory of God. More than that, we rejoice in our sufferings, knowing that suffering produces endurance, and endurance produces character, and character produces hope, and hope does not disappoint us, because God's love has been poured into our hearts through the Holy Spirit who has been given to us.

While we were yet helpless, at the right time Christ died for the ungodly. Why, one will hardly die for a righteous man — though perhaps for a good man one will dare even to die. But God shows his love for us in that while we were yet sinners Christ died for us. Since, therefore, we are now justified by his blood, much more shall we be saved by him from the wrath of God. For if while we were enemies we were reconciled to God by the death of his Son, much more, now that we are reconciled, shall we be saved by his life. Not only so, but we also rejoice in God through our Lord Jesus Christ, through whom we have now received our reconciliation.

— ROMANS 5:1-11

God Is With Us When We Suffer

Likewise the Spirit helps us in our weakness; for we do not know how to pray as we ought, but the Spirit himself intercedes for us with sighs too deep for words. And he who searches the hearts of men knows what is the mind of the Spirit, because the Spirit intercedes for the saints according to the will of God.

We know that in everything God works for good with those who love him, who are called according to his purpose. For those whom he foreknew he also predestined to be conformed to the image of his Son, in order that he might be the first-born among many brethren. And those whom he predestined he also called; and those whom he called he also justified; and those whom he justified he also glorified.

What then shall we say to this? If God is for us, who is against us? He who did not spare his own Son but gave him up for us all, will he not also give us all things with him? Who shall bring any charge against God's elect? It is God who justifies; who is to condemn? Is it Christ Jesus, who died, yes, who was raised from the dead, who is at the right hand of God, who indeed intercedes for us? Who shall separate us from the love of Christ? Shall tribulation, or distress, or persecution, or famine, or nakedness, or peril, or sword? As it is written,

"For your sake we are being killed all the day long;
we are regarded as sheep to be slaughtered."

No, in all these things we are more than conquerors through him who loved us. For I am sure that neither death, nor life, nor angels, nor principalities, nor

things present, nor things to come, nor powers, nor
height, nor depth, nor anything else in all creation, will
be able to separate us from the love of God in Christ
Jesus our Lord.

— ROMANS 8:26-39

Meditating on Christ's Suffering

My God, my God, why have you forsaken me?
  Why are you so far from helping me, from the
    words of my groaning?
O my God, I cry by day, but you do not answer;
  and by night, but find no rest.

Yet you are holy,
  enthroned on the praises of Israel.
In you our fathers trusted;
  they trusted, and you delivered them.
To you they cried, and were saved;
  in you they trusted, and were not disappointed.

But I am a worm, and no man;
  scorned by men, and despised by the people.
All who see me mock at me,
  they make mouths at me, they wag their heads;
"He committed his cause to the LORD; let him deliver him,
  let him rescue him, for he delights in him!"

Yet you are he who took me from the womb;
  you kept me safe upon my mother's breasts.
Upon you was I cast from my birth,

and since my mother bore me you have been my
     God.
Be not far from me,
    for trouble is near
    and there is none to help.

Many bulls encompass me,
    strong bulls of Bashan surround me;
they open wide their mouths at me,
    like a ravening and roaring lion.

I am poured out like water,
    and all my bones are out of joint;
my heart is like wax,
    it is melted within my breast;
my strength is dried up like a potsherd,
    and my tongue cleaves to my jaws;
    you lay me in the dust of death.

Yes, dogs are round about me;
    a company of evildoers encircle me;
    they have pierced my hands and feet —
I can count all my bones —
    they stare and gloat over me;
they divide my garments among them,
    and for my clothing they cast lots.

But you, O Lord, be not far off!
    O my help, hasten to my aid!
Deliver my soul from the sword,
    my life from the power of the dog!

Save me from the mouth of the lion,
   my afflicted soul from the horns of the wild oxen!

I will tell of your name to my brethren;
   in the midst of the congregation I will praise you:
You who fear the LORD, praise him!
   all you sons of Jacob, glorify him,
   and stand in awe of him, all you sons of Israel!
For he has not despised or abhorred
   the affliction of the afflicted;
and he has not hid his face from him,
   but has heard, when he cried to him.

From you comes my praise in the great congregation;
   my vows I will pay before those who fear him.
The afflicted shall eat and be satisfied;
   those who seek him shall praise the LORD!
   May your hearts live for ever!

All the ends of the earth shall remember
   and turn to the LORD;
and all the families of the nations
   shall worship before him.
For dominion belongs to the LORD,
   and he rules over the nations.

Yes, to him shall all the proud of the earth bow down;
   before him shall bow all who go down to the dust,
   and he who cannot keep himself alive.
Posterity shall serve him;

men shall tell of the Lord to the coming
    generation,
and proclaim his deliverance to a people yet unborn,
    that he has wrought it.

Psalm 22

A Prayer for God's Mercy

Out of the depths I cry to you, O Lord!
    Lord, hear my voice!
Let your ears be attentive
    to the voice of my supplications!

If you, O Lord, should mark iniquities,
    Lord, who could stand?
But there is forgiveness with you,
    that you may be revered.

I wait for the Lord, my soul waits,
    and in his word I hope;
my soul waits for the Lord
    more than watchmen for the morning,
    more than watchmen for the morning.

O Israel, hope in the Lord!
    For with the Lord there is mercy,
    and with him is plenteous redemption.
And he will redeem Israel
    from all his iniquities.

— Psalm 130

A Plea for God's Help

Bless the LORD, O my soul,
>and all that is within me,
>bless his holy name!
Bless the LORD, O my soul,
>and forget not all his benefits —
who forgives all your iniquity,
>who heals all your diseases,
who redeems your life from the Pit,
>who crowns you with mercy and compassion,
who satisfies you with good as long as you live
>so that your youth is renewed like the eagle's.

The LORD works vindication
>and justice for all who are oppressed.
He made known his ways to Moses,
>his acts to the people of Israel.
The LORD is merciful and gracious,
>slow to anger and abounding in mercy.
He will not always chide,
>nor will he keep his anger for ever.
He does not deal with us according to our sins,
>nor repay us according to our iniquities.
For as the heavens are high above the earth,
>so great is his mercy toward those who fear
>>him;
as far as the east is from the west,
>so far does he remove our transgressions from us.
As a father pities his children,
>so the LORD pities those who fear him.

For he knows our frame;
 he remembers that we are dust.

As for man, his days are like grass;
 he flourishes like a flower of the field;
for the wind passes over it, and it is gone,
 and its place knows it no more.
But the mercy of the LORD is from everlasting to everlasting
 upon those who fear him,
 and his righteousness to children's children,
to those who keep his covenant
 and remember to do his commandments.

The LORD has established his throne in the heavens,
 and his kingdom rules over all.
Bless the LORD, O you his angels,
 you mighty ones who do his word,
 harkening to the voice of his word!
Bless the LORD, all his hosts,
 his ministers that do his will!
Bless the LORD, all his works,
 in all places of his dominion.
Bless the LORD, O my soul!

— PSALM 103

The Memorare

Remember, O most gracious Virgin Mary, that never was it known that anyone who fled to your protection, implored your help, or sought your intercession was left unaided.

Inspired by this confidence, I fly unto you, O Virgin of virgins, my mother; to you do I come, before you I stand, sinful and sorrowful.

O Mother of the Word Incarnate, despise not my petitions, but in your mercy hear and answer me. Amen.

Prayer to St. Michael

St. Michael the Archangel, defend us in battle; be our defense against the wickedness and snares of the devil. May God rebuke him, we humbly pray; and do you, O Prince of the heavenly host, by the power of God, thrust into hell Satan and the other evil spirits who prowl about the world seeking the ruin of souls. Amen.

Litany of the Holy Guardian Angel

Lord, have mercy on us. **Lord, have mercy on us.**
Christ, have mercy on us. **Christ, have mercy on us.**
Lord, have mercy on us. **Lord, have mercy on us.**
Christ, hear us. **Christ, hear us.**
Christ, graciously hear us.

God, the Father of heaven,   **Have mercy on us.**
God, the Son, Redeemer of the world...
God, the Holy Spirit...
Holy Trinity, One God...

Holy Mary, Queen of Angels,   **Pray for us.**
Holy Angel, my guardian...
Holy Angel, my prince...
Holy Angel, my monitor...
Holy Angel, my counselor...
Holy Angel, my defender...
Holy Angel, my steward...
Holy Angel, my friend...
Holy Angel, my consoler...
Holy Angel, my patron...
Holy Angel, my teacher...
Holy Angel, my leader...
Holy Angel, my intercessor...
Holy Angel, my protector...
Holy Angel, my defender...
Holly Angel, my comforter...
Holy Angel, my brother...
Holy Angel, my preacher...
Holy Angel, my shepherd...
Holy Angel, my witness...
Holy Angel, my helper...
Holy Angel, my watcher...
Holy Angel, my negotiator...
Holy Angel, my conductor...
Holy Angel, my preserver...

Holy Angel, my instructor...   **Pray for us.**
Holy Angel, my enlightener...

Holy Angel, guard and keep me.

From every sin,   **Guard and preserve us.**
From every danger...
From every snare of the devil...
From every enemy, visible and invisible...
From pestilence, hunger, and war...
From sluggishness in the service of God...
From sadness and anxiety...
From hardness of heart...
From the unworthy reception of the Most Holy Body
    and Blood of the Lord...
From a sudden and unprovided death...
From the eternal death...

Lamb of God, who takes away the sins of the world,
              Spare us, O Lord.
Lamb of God, who takes away the sins of the world,
              Graciously hear us, O Lord.
Lamb of God, who takes away the sins of the world,
              Have mercy on us.

Let us pray: Almighty and eternal God, who has created me in your image, though unworthy that I am, and has assigned your holy angel as my guardian, grant me, your servant, that I may happily pass over the dangers of every evil, both of body and soul, and after the course of this life come to eternal joy. Through Christ our Lord. Amen.